Successful Stock S[

John James Butler

Alpha Editions

This edition published in 2024

ISBN : 9789364734868

Design and Setting By
Alpha Editions
www.alphaedis.com
Email - info@alphaedis.com

As per information held with us this book is in Public Domain.
This book is a reproduction of an important historical work. Alpha Editions uses the best technology to reproduce historical work in the same manner it was first published to preserve its original nature. Any marks or number seen are left intentionally to preserve its true form.

Contents

PART ONE INTRODUCTORY CHAPTERS .... - 1 -

CHAPTER I. THE PURPOSE OF THIS BOOK .... - 3 -

CHAPTER II. WHAT IS SPECULATION? .... - 4 -

CHAPTER III. SOME TERMS EXPLAINED .... - 6 -

CHAPTER IV. A CORRECT BASIS FOR SPECULATING .... - 8 -

PART TWO WHAT and WHEN TO BUY and SELL .... - 11 -

CHAPTER V. WHAT STOCKS TO BUY .... - 13 -

CHAPTER VI. WHAT STOCKS NOT TO BUY .... - 14 -

CHAPTER VII. WHEN TO BUY STOCKS .... - 16 -

FOOTNOTES: .... - 17 -

CHAPTER VIII. WHEN NOT TO BUY STOCKS .... - 18 -

CHAPTER IX. WHEN TO SELL STOCKS .... - 19 -

PART THREE INFLUENCES AFFECTING STOCK PRICES ....- 21 -

CHAPTER X. MOVEMENTS IN STOCK PRICES ....- 23 -

CHAPTER XI. MAJOR MOVEMENTS IN PRICES ....- 24 -

CHAPTER XII. THE MONEY MARKET AND STOCK PRICES ....- 26 -

CHAPTER XIII. MINOR MOVEMENTS IN PRICES ....- 27 -

CHAPTER XIV. TECHNICAL CONDITIONS ....- 28 -

CHAPTER XV. MANIPULATIONS ....- 29 -

PART FOUR TOPICS OF INTEREST TO SPECULATORS ....- 33 -

CHAPTER XVI. MARGINAL TRADING ....- 35 -

CHAPTER XVII. SHORT SELLING ....- 37 -

CHAPTER XVIII. BUCKET SHOPS ....- 39 -

CHAPTER XIX. CHOOSING A BROKER ....- 40 -

CHAPTER XX. PUTS AND CALLS ....- 41 -

CHAPTER XXI. STOP LOSS ORDERS ....- 42 -

PART FIVE CONCLUDING CHAPTERS ....- 45 -

CHAPTER XXII. THE DESIRE TO SPECULATE .... - 47 -

CHAPTER XXIII. TWO KINDS OF TRADERS .... - 50 -

CHAPTER XXIV. POSSIBILITIES OF PROFIT .... - 52 -

CHAPTER XXV. MARKET INFORMATION .... - 54 -

CHAPTER XXVI. SUCCESSFUL SPECULATION .... - 58 -

FOOTNOTES: .... - 61 -

PART ONE
INTRODUCTORY CHAPTERS

CHAPTER I.
THE PURPOSE OF THIS BOOK

This book is written for the purpose of giving our clients some ideas of the fundamental principles that guide us when we select stocks for them to buy, but these principles are valuable to every person who trades in listed stocks or in any other kind of speculative stocks.

First of all, we want you to get a clear conception of the meaning of the word speculation, which is explained in the next chapter. Our purpose is to protect you against losses as well as to enable you to make profits, and it is very important that you understand how to provide for safety in your speculating.

It is a well known fact that there are tremendous losses in stock speculation, but we claim that almost all of these losses would be avoided if all speculators were guided by the principles expounded in this book.

"What" and "When" are two very important words in stock speculation, and we cannot urge upon you too strongly to study carefully Chapters V. to IX.

Chapters X. to XV. tell you much about the influences that affect the prices of stocks, a knowledge of which should also be a guide to you in making your selections.

Perhaps the most important chapter in the entire book is XXV., on Market Information. A careful reading of this chapter should convince you that much of the prevailing information about the stock market is misleading. That fact alone accounts for many of the losses in stock speculation.

It has been our aim to state all facts briefly. The entire book is not long, and it will not require much of your time to read it through carefully. We are sure you will get many ideas from it that will help you.

CHAPTER II.
WHAT IS SPECULATION?

To speculate is to theorize about something that is uncertain. We can speculate about anything that is uncertain, but we use the word "speculation" in this book with particular reference to the buying and selling of stocks and bonds for the purpose of making a profit. When people buy stocks and bonds for the income they get from them and the amount of that income is fixed, they are said to invest and not to speculate. In nearly all investments there is also an element of speculation, because the market price of investments is subject to change. "Investment" also conveys the idea of holding for some time whatever you have purchased, while speculation conveys the idea of selling for a quick profit rather than holding for income.

To the minds of most people, the word "speculation" conveys the thought of risk, and many people think it means great risk. The dictionary gives for one of the meanings of speculation, "a risky investment for large profit," but speculation need not necessarily be risky at all. The author of this book once used the expression, "stock speculating with safety," and he was severely criticized by a certain financial magazine. Evidently the editor of that magazine thought that "speculating" and "safety" were contradictory terms, but the expression is perfectly correct. Stock speculating with safety is possible.

Of course, we all know that the word "safety" is seldom used in an absolute sense. We frequently read such expressions as: "The elevators in modern office buildings are run with safety." "It is possible to cross the ocean with safety." "You can travel from New York to San Francisco in a railroad train with safety." And yet accidents do occur and people do lose their lives in elevators, steamships, and railroad trains. Because serious accidents are comparatively rare, we use the word "safety."

In like manner it is possible to purchase stocks sometimes when it is almost certain that the purchaser will make a profit, and that is "stock speculating with safety." When Liberty Bonds were selling in the 80's, many people bought them for speculation. They were not taking any risk, except the slight risk that the market price might go still lower before it would go higher, and that did not involve any risk for those who knew they could hold them. The fact that the market prices of Liberty Bonds would advance was based upon an economic law that never fails. That law is that when interest rates go up, the market prices of bonds go down, and when interest rates go down, the market prices of bonds go up. When Liberty Bonds were selling in the 80's, interest rates were so very high, it was certain that they would come down. That the market prices of Liberty Bonds would go up was also certain, but nobody could tell how much they would go up in a given time. It was that element of uncertainty that made them speculative, and not that there was any doubt about the fact that the market prices of them would go up. Buying Liberty Bonds at that time was speculating with safety. If you read this book with understanding, you will know much about speculating with safety.

CHAPTER III.
SOME TERMS EXPLAINED

There are certain terms used in connection with stock speculation that are very familiar to those who come in contact with stock brokers, and yet are not always familiar to those who do business by mail. Undoubtedly the majority of our readers are familiar with these terms, but we give these definitions for the benefit of the few who are not familiar with them.

Trader: A person who buys and sells stocks is usually referred to as a trader. The word probably originated when it was customary to trade one stock for another and later was used to refer to a person who sold one stock and bought another. He was a trader; but the person who buys stocks for a profit and sells them and takes his profit when he gets an opportunity, may not be a trader in the strict sense of the word. However, for convenience, we use the word "trader" in this book to refer to any one who buys or sells stocks.

Speculator: This word refers to a person who buys stocks for profit, with the expectation of selling at a higher price, without reference to the earnings of the stock. He may sell first, with the expectation of buying at a lower price, as explained in Chapter XVII. on "Short Selling." In many cases where we use the word "trader," it would be more correct to use the word "speculator."

Investor: An investor differs from a speculator in the fact that he buys stocks or bonds with the expectation of holding them for some time for the income to be derived from them, without reference to their speculative possibilities. We believe that investors always should give some consideration to the speculative possibilities of their purchases. It frequently is possible to get speculative profits without increase of risk or loss of income.

Bull: One who believes that the market price of stocks will advance is called a bull. Of course, it is possible to be a bull in one stock and a bear in another. The word is used very frequently with reference to the market, a bull market meaning a rising market.

Bear: The opposite of a bull is a bear. It refers to a person who believes that the market value of stocks will decline, and a bear market is a declining market.

Lambs: "Lambs" refers to that part of the public that knows so little about stock speculating that they lose all their money sooner or later. The bulls and bears get them going and coming. If the lambs would read this book carefully, they would discover reasons why they lose their money.

Long and Short: Those who **own** stocks are said to be long, and those who **owe** stocks are said to be short. Short selling is explained in Chapter XVII.

Odd Lot: Stocks on exchanges are sold in certain lots. On the New York Stock Exchange, 100 shares is a lot; and on the Consolidated Stock Exchange, 10 shares is a lot. Less than these amounts is an odd lot. When you sell an odd lot you usually get 1/8 less than the market price; and when you buy an odd lot, you usually pay 1/8 more than the market price; that is, 1/8 of a dollar on each share where prices are quoted in dollars.

Point: It is a common expression to say that a stock went up or down a point, which means a dollar in a stock that is quoted in dollars, but a cent in a stock that is quoted in cents, as many of the stocks are on the New York Curb. In cotton quotations, a point is 1/100 part of a cent. For instance, if cotton is quoted at 18.12, it means 18 cents and 12/100 of a cent per pound, and if it went up 30 points the quotation would be 18.42.

Reaction: Every person who has traded in listed stocks probably is familiar with this word. It means to act in an opposite direction, but it is used especially to refer to a decline in the price of a stock that has been going up.

Rally: "Rally" is the opposite of the sense in which "reaction" usually is used. When a stock is going down and it turns and goes up, it is called a rally.

Commitment: This term is used referring to a purchase of stock. It is more commonly used by investment bankers when they contract to buy an issue, but the term sometimes is used by traders.

Floating Supply: The stock of a company that is in the hands of that part of the public who is likely to sell, is referred to as floating supply.

CHAPTER IV.
A CORRECT BASIS FOR SPECULATING

We maintain that there is only one basis upon which successful speculation can be carried on continually; that is, never to buy a security unless it is selling at a price below that which is warranted by assets, earning power, and prospective future earning power.

There are many influences that affect the movements of stock prices, which are referred to in subsequent chapters. All of these should be studied and understood, but they should be used as secondary factors in relation to the value of the stock in which you are trading.

If the market price of any stock is far below its intrinsic value and there is no reason why the future should bring about a change in this value that will decrease it, then you may be certain that important influences are working against the market price of the stock for the time being. In the course of time the market price will go up towards the real value. This matter will be more fully explained in subsequent chapters.

You always should keep in mind the fact that when you buy a stock at a higher price than its intrinsic value, you are taking a risk. The stock may have great future possibilities, but it is risky to buy stocks when present assets and earnings do not warrant their market prices, no matter how attractive prospective future earnings may appear. However, the possibilities of profit sometimes are so great that one is justified in taking this risk.

It is our belief that the majority of traders buy stocks because they are active in the market and somebody said they were a good buy, even though the real values may not be nearly as much as the market prices.

As an example of this kind of trading, we want to call your attention to a news item that appeared in a New York paper. It stated that on April 1st, some brokers in Detroit, as an April Fool joke, gave out a tip to buy A. F. P., meaning April Fool Preferred, but when asked what it meant, replied "American Fire Protection." Of course, there was no such stock, but there was active trading in it until the joke was discovered. Evidently it is not necessary to list a stock on the Detroit Stock Exchange in order to trade in it.

This story may or may not be true, but we believe the statement that people trade in stocks they do not know anything about is true. You should be careful not to buy a stock merely because somebody says it is a good thing to buy, unless the person making the statement is in the business of giving information on stocks, because it may be only a rumor with no substantial basis. Of course, if many people act on the rumor, there will be active trading in the stock, and it is frequently for that purpose that such rumors are started.

PART TWO
WHAT and WHEN TO BUY and SELL

CHAPTER V.
WHAT STOCKS TO BUY

In deciding what stocks to buy, it is well to consider first the classes of stocks, and then what particular stocks you should buy in the classes you select. We would first of all divide all stocks into two classes, those listed on the New York Stock Exchange and those not listed on the New York Stock Exchange. As a rule, it is better to buy stocks listed on the New York Stock Exchange, although there are frequent exceptions to this rule.

Then, the stocks listed on the New York Stock Exchange may be divided into classes, such as railroad stocks, public utility stocks, motor stocks, tire stocks, oil stocks, copper stocks, gold stocks, and so forth. At certain times certain stocks are in a much more favorable condition than at other times. In 1919, when the industrial stocks were selling at a very high price, the public utility stocks and gold stocks were selling low, because it was impossible to increase incomes in proportion to the increase in operating costs. But since the beginning of 1921, the condition of these two classes of stocks has been improving and the market has reflected that improvement.

At the time of this writing (early in April, 1922) we are recommending the stocks of only a very few manufacturing companies; but we are recommending a number (not all) of the railroad and public utility stocks, and a few specially selected stocks among the other classes.

In every instance, when you make a selection, you should consider the company's assets, present earnings, and prospective future earnings, and then take into consideration all the influences that affect price movements, as explained in subsequent chapters.

CHAPTER VI.
WHAT STOCKS NOT TO BUY

A great deal more can be said about stocks you should not buy than about stocks you should buy, because the list is very much larger.

Stocks not listed on the New York Stock Exchange, as a rule, should not be bought by a careful speculator, but as stated in the previous chapter, there are exceptions to that rule. Billions of dollars have been lost in the past by buying stocks that have become worthless. A few years ago a list of defunct securities was compiled, and it took two large volumes in which to enumerate them. New ones have been added to them every year. Therefore, it is very important that you should give careful thought to the subject of what stocks **not** to buy.

Nearly all promotion stocks (stocks in new companies) are a failure. An extremely small percentage of them are very successful, and the successful ones are referred to in the advertising of the new ones; but, on the basis of average, the chances are you will lose your money entirely in promotion stocks. We believe that most of the promotion companies are started in perfectly good faith, although some of them are swindles from the beginning; but no matter how honest and well meaning the organizers are, the chances of success are against them. Therefore, we say that promotion stocks should not be bought by the ordinary man who is looking for a good speculation, because his chances of making a large profit with a minimum risk are very much better when he buys stocks listed on the New York Stock Exchange and uses good judgment in doing so.

Among the listed stocks there are many you should not buy. First of all, eliminate them by classes. Do not buy the classes of stocks that are selling too high now. You may say that there are some exceptions in all classes. That may or may not be so, but in any event, you have a better chance of profiting by confining most of your purchases to the classes of stocks that are in the most favorable position.

As a rule, when stocks are first listed, they sell much higher than they do a short time afterwards. Of course, that is not always true. It is more likely to be true when a stock is listed during a very active market, when prices are more easily influenced by publicity. The high price of it is usually due to the fact that publicity is given to it, and as soon as the effect of this publicity wears off, the market price of the stock declines.

It is a good rule never to buy stocks that brokers urge you to buy. Your own common sense ought to tell you that a stock that is advertised extensively by brokers is likely to sell up in price while the advertising is going on and will drop in price just as soon as the advertising stops.

Many people notice that and they think they can profit by buying when the advertising starts and sell out when they get a good profit, but the majority of them lose money. The stock may not respond to the advertising, or if it does go up, they may wait too long before selling. Those who do sell and make 200% or 300% profit in a very short time are almost sure to lose it all in an effort to repeat the transaction. Many of those who read this know it is true from their own experience.

You should leave such stocks strictly alone. You may win once or twice, but you are sure to lose if you keep it up. As a rule stocks of this kind have very little value and the brokers who boost them make their own money from the losses of their foolish followers.

CHAPTER VII.
WHEN TO BUY STOCKS

Stocks should be bought when they are cheap. By being cheap, we mean that the market price is much less than the intrinsic value. In Chapters X. to XV. we talk about influences that affect the price movements of stocks. By studying these carefully you should be able to decide when stocks generally are cheap. Of course, not all stocks are cheap at the same time, but the majority of listed stocks do go up and down at the same time, as a rule.

At the time of this writing (in the early part of April, 1922) there are a great many stocks listed on the New York Stock Exchange that are selling at prices much less than their intrinsic values, but there are some stocks that should not be bought now, nor at any other time. There are some stocks listed on the New York Stock Exchange now that perhaps have no intrinsic value and never will have any. Nevertheless we consider that right now[1] is one of the times for buying stocks. There are unusual bargains to be had, although keen discrimination is necessary in order to be able to pick out the bargains.

As a usual thing, it is a good time to buy stocks when nearly everybody wants to sell them. When general business conditions are bad, trading on the stock exchanges very light, and everybody you meet appears to be pessimistic, then we advise you to look for bargains in stocks. The last six months of 1921 was an unusually good time for buying stocks.

It is well known that the large interests accumulate stocks at such times. They buy only when the stocks are offered at a low price and try not to buy enough at any one time to give an appearance of activity in the market, but they buy continually when the market is very dull. It seems to be characteristic of human nature to think that business conditions are going to continue just as they are. When business is bad, nearly everybody thinks business will be bad for a long time, and when business is good, nearly everybody thinks business will be good almost indefinitely. As a matter of fact, conditions are always changing. It never is possible for either extremely good times nor for extremely bad times to continue indefinitely.

You can buy stocks cheaper when there is very little demand for them, and you should arrange your affairs so as to be prepared to buy at such times.

FOOTNOTES:

[1] In our advisory Letter of April 25, 1922, we advised our clients to refrain from margin buying for a while, because the market was advancing too rapidly. Shortly after that there was a decided reaction in the market.

CHAPTER VIII.
WHEN NOT TO BUY STOCKS

There are times when stocks should not be bought, and that is when nearly all stocks have advanced beyond their real values. It is doubtful if there ever is a time when all stocks have advanced beyond their real values, but when the great majority of stocks have so advanced, there is likely to be a general decline in all stock prices. The stocks that are not selling too high will decline some in sympathy with the others. Therefore, there are times when we advise our clients not to buy any stocks.

Some organizations giving advice in regard to the buying of stocks, advise their clients to refrain entirely from buying for periods of a year or longer, but we think it is seldom advisable to refrain entirely from buying for any great length of time. There usually are some good opportunities if you watch carefully for them. It is our business to watch for these opportunities and tell our clients about them.

There are also times when the technical condition of the market is such that we advise our clients to refrain from buying for a while. See Chapter XIV.

CHAPTER IX.
WHEN TO SELL STOCKS

You should sell stocks when the market price is too high. That is a general rule, but it is necessary for you to study all the influences affecting stock prices to be able to decide more accurately when you should sell your stocks. We give you, in future chapters, much more information on judging the markets.

Another general rule, is to sell stocks when nearly everybody is buying them. It is a well known fact that the great majority of people buy stocks near the top and sell near the bottom. Naturally when everybody is optimistic, stocks will sell up high, but sooner or later they will come down again, and when everything looks very promising is a good time to sell. It is better to lose a little of the profit that you might have made by holding on longer than not to be on the safe side. The man who tries to sell at the top nearly always loses, because stocks seldom sell as high as it is predicted they will, or, in other words, the prediction of higher prices is advanced more rapidly than the prices.

We remember reading in 1916, when U. S. Steel sold up around $136 a share, a prediction that it was going to sell up to $1000 a share. Probably many people who read such news items consider them seriously. Of course, that was a most exaggerated prediction, but during the extreme activity of a bull market, it seems that nearly everybody is talking in exaggerated terms of optimism. That is why most traders seldom ever take their profits in a bull market. They wait until stock prices start to come down, and then they are likely to think there will be rallies, and keep on waiting until they lose all their profits.

On the other hand, some people make the mistake of selling too soon. Just because your purchase shows a liberal profit is no reason why you should sell. The stock may have been very cheap when you bought it. In 1920, Peoples Gas sold below $30. Those who bought it then were able to double their money by the close of 1921, and many sold out and took their profits. Of course, if they invested the proceeds in other stocks that were just starting upward, they may not have lost anything, but there was no particular reason for selling Peoples Gas at that time. The public utilities generally were coming into their own, and nearly all of them were regarded by economic students as having unusual opportunities for profit.

Then again, it is not always a mistake to sell a stock in order to get funds to put into something else that seems more promising, even though the stock you sell is likely to go much higher.

It is very important that you should try to sell your stocks at the right time. That is the main thing to keep in mind and it is better to sell too soon than too late. Don't be too greedy and hold on for a big profit. Read Chapter XXIV. on the "Possibilities of Profit."

PART THREE
INFLUENCES AFFECTING STOCK PRICES

CHAPTER X.
MOVEMENTS IN STOCK PRICES

It is due to the fact that stock prices constantly move up or down that speculation is possible. Sometimes certain stocks remain almost at a standstill for a long period of time, but at least a part of the stocks listed on the Exchanges move either up or down. If one always could tell just what way they were going to move, it would be comparatively easy to make a fortune within a short time.

In the last twenty years, a great deal of time and money has been spent by statistical organizations in checking up statistics for the purpose of ascertaining a definite basis upon which to predict future movements in stock prices. Several of these organizations use very different statistics upon which to base their conclusions, and yet their conclusions are very similar. They have proved beyond any question of doubt that some of these movements are clearly indicated by laws that never fail.

We do not attempt in this book to explain the fundamental statistics upon which the predictions of business cycles are based, but in the next five chapters we explain some of the influences that affect the movements in stock prices. Read these chapters very carefully, for your success in stock speculation will depend very largely upon your correct prediction of these movements.

CHAPTER XI.
MAJOR MOVEMENTS IN PRICES

Stock prices move up and down in cycles. These are the major movements in prices, but there may be many minor movements up and down within the major movements. These stock price movements nearly always precede a change in business conditions; that is, an upward movement in stock prices is an indication that business conditions are going to improve, and a downward movement in stock prices is an indication that business conditions are going to get worse.

At the present writing, we are in a period of improvement. Stock prices began to go up in August, 1921. The upward movement has been slow, but gradual. In a period of seven months, forty representative stocks show an upward movement of about 20 points, although business has not shown much improvement. A steady upward movement in stock prices is a sure sign that business conditions are beginning to improve, even though that improvement is not noticeable.

These major stock movements are not an exact duplicate of any previous ones, and it is impossible to tell how long they will last or just what course they will take. Certain influences could change a period of improvement into a period of prosperity very quickly.

A period of prosperity is noted for high prices, high wages, and increasing production in all lines. Everybody is optimistic. Most people spend their money freely, and that makes times better. As prices go up and business increases, more money is required in business and interest rates go up. As a consequence, when interest rates go up, bond prices go down. During this period, speculative stocks are selling at their highest prices; and under the influence of this movement, many stocks that have no actual value sell up at high prices. Of course, wise speculators sell all their stocks during this period.

Following a period of prosperity comes a period of decline. The first sign of it usually is a severe break in the stock market. At that time general business is running along at top speed and there is no sign of a let-up, but this break in the stock market should be a warning. Most people think the break is merely a temporary reaction—they may refer to it as a HEALTHY reaction—and they start buying stocks again, and put the market up, but it does not go up as high as it was before the break occurred. When stock prices do not rally beyond the prices at which they were before the break occurred, it is a sign that the turning point has been reached and that the bear market has started, although the majority of people do not realize this until a long time afterwards.

Next comes a period of depression, when we have low prices, low wages, hard times, tight money, and many commercial failures. Many people who lost all their money during the speculation period, become thrifty and economize during the period of depression, and start in to save again. Nearly everybody is pessimistic during this period. Trading on the Stock Exchange is irregular and as a rule very light.

This is the time to get stock bargains, but the general public as a rule doesn't take advantage of it. People are scared and think prices will go still lower. The big interests accumulate stocks during this period, and sell them during the period of prosperity.

CHAPTER XII.
THE MONEY MARKET AND STOCK PRICES

Perhaps no other one thing influences the movement of stock prices so much, in a large way, as money conditions. It is impossible to have a big bull market without plenty of money. During a bull market nearly all stocks are bought on margin, which is explained in Chapter XVI. This makes it necessary for brokers to borrow large sums of money. When money is tight, it is impossible to get enough to carry on a large movement in stocks.

You will see, therefore, that the Federal Reserve Bank has it in its power to regulate the stock market to some extent. In 1919 speculation was carried very much further than it should have been, but undoubtedly it would have been much worse had the Federal Reserve Bank not raised interest rates and urged member banks to withdraw money from Wall Street. While there was considerable criticism of that action, it certainly was a good thing for the entire country.

In a period of depression, the banks accumulate money, and there always is an abundance of money at the beginning of a bull market. During a period of prosperity the banks' reserves decrease and their loans increase. When you see these reserves go down to a very low point, it is usually time for you to sell your stocks.

CHAPTER XIII.
MINOR MOVEMENTS IN PRICES

Within the major movements of stock prices, there always are several minor movements, which are caused by various influences. One of the important causes is the technical condition of the market. Another cause might be called a psychological one. When stocks are moving up steadily in a bull market, people closely connected with the market expect a reaction and watch for it. The newspapers predict it. Consequently, there is sufficient let-up in buying to allow the pressure of selling by the bears to bring it about. However, the desire to buy during reactions is so general, many people rush in to buy and this buying, in addition to the covering by the shorts, puts the market up again; and if conditions are favorable for a bull market, prices will go up much higher than they were before.

In like manner, we have rallies in bear markets. Of course the professional bears sell during these rallies, with the expectation of buying later at a cheaper price.

These minor price changes mean more to the majority of traders than the major movements. The major movements are so slow that people get out of patience, and yet those who are guided only by the major movements are operating on a much safer basis. We believe that a greater amount of money can be made, with a minimum risk, by being guided principally by the major movements, while taking advantage of the minor movements in a minor way. However, stocks do not move uniformly and there frequently is an opportunity to buy some particular stock at a bargain when nearly all stocks are selling too high. We try to pick out these opportunities for our clients.

Reports of earnings by various companies influence stock prices, as does also the paying of extra dividends or the passing up of dividends. A peculiar psychological influence is noticed when a company declares an extra dividend. The price of the stock usually goes up, while as a matter of fact the intrinsic value of the stock is decreased by the amount of this dividend; and sometimes it is advisable to sell a stock shortly after an advance in its dividend rate.

CHAPTER XIV.
TECHNICAL CONDITIONS

Technical conditions refer to the conditions that usually affect the supply and demand, such as short interests, floating supply, and stop loss orders.

It is sometimes said that supply and demand must be equal or else there could not be any sales, but that is not so. There are always some people who are willing to sell at some price above the market who will not sell at the market; and when the demand for stock is greater than the supply, it goes up until it is supplied by some of these people who are holding it at a higher price.

It works the same way when the supply is greater than the demand. There are always some people who will buy at some price below the market. Therefore, when the supply is greater than the demand prices must go down.

A stock may have an intrinsic value of $100 a share and yet be selling at $50 a share, and it can never sell higher than $50 until all stock that is offered at that price is bought.

However, you should keep this in mind: if the real value is $100 a share, sooner or later the market price will approach that figure. That is why we so strongly urge our clients to buy stocks that have actual values, or at least prospective values far greater than their market prices, and either to buy them outright or margin them very heavily, and then hold them until the prices do go up.

Of course, when one finds that a mistake has been made, the sooner one sells and takes a loss the better.

CHAPTER XV.
MANIPULATIONS

Stock prices are influenced largely by manipulation. Years ago when the volume of trading on the New York Stock Exchange was small compared with what it is today, it was possible to influence the entire market by manipulation, but it would be very difficult to do that today. It is only certain stocks that are manipulated; but if conditions are favorable, many other stocks may be influenced by them.

There are different kinds of manipulation. One is for the insiders of a company to give out unfavorable news about their company if they want the price of the stock to go down, so that they can buy it in; or to give out very favorable news if they want the price to go up, so that they can sell out. This method is not practiced now to the extent that it was years ago. Public opinion is strongly opposed to it, and we believe business men are acquiring a higher standard of business ethics. Methods of this kind are legal but they are morally reprehensible.

Another method of manipulation is the forming of pools to buy in the stock of a company and force it up. If the market price of a stock is far below its real value, we believe it is justifiable for a pool to force it up, but the ordinary pool is merely a scheme to rob the public.

There are four periods to the operation of such pools. First is the period of accumulation. A number of large holders of stock in a certain company will pool their stock, all agreeing not to sell except from the pool, in which all benefit proportionately. Then they give out bad news about the company. That is very easy to do, because financial writers usually accept the news that is given to them without much investigation, especially writers on daily papers, because they have not the time to investigate. Their copy must be ready in a few hours after they get the information. See Chapter XXV. on "Market Information" for fuller explanation of the reason why financial news usually is misleading. The manipulators of stock prices can have financial news "made to order."

When the general public reads this news and sees the stock going down, many of them get discouraged and sell. It is just the time they should not sell, but it is a well known fact that the majority of people do in the stock market just what they should not do. The more they sell the more the price goes down, and the pool operators accumulate the stock.

Having secured all the stock they want, they give out good news and continue to buy the stock until it starts to go up. The public reads this favorable news, and seeing the stock go up, will go into the market and buy, which puts it up higher. All the time financial writers are supplying good news about the stock and the public buys it. After they have sold all of it, the public may still be anxious for more, and the pool operators may go short of the stock. Then they will begin giving out bad news, so that they can buy in stock at a lower price to cover their short interests.

After that they have very little interest in the market. If it is declining too fast, they may support it occasionally by buying some stock and giving out some favorable news. That will make the market rally and they will sell out the newly acquired stock near the top of the rally.

Manipulations of this kind appear to be going on nearly all the time, and there does not seem to be any limit to the number of suckers who fall for them. But then, one can't blame the public when you realize how thoroughly unreliable is most of the market information given to them.

Still another kind of manipulation is "one-man" manipulation, where one man controls companies, which are known as "one-man" companies. Usually the directors of these companies are friends or employees of his, and in many instances he has their resignations in his possession, so that they must do whatever he wants them to do. Owing to the strict rules of the New York Stock Exchange, it is rather difficult for such manipulations to be carried on there. But there have been many of them on the New York Curb. When the Curb was operating on the street and was not under very much control, manipulations of this kind were very frequent.

As an example, suppose a man of this kind has a mining company. When he wants the stock to go up, he sends the stockholders a great deal of information about the work at the mine, and perhaps sends them a telegram when a new vein of rich ore is found. The stockholders rush in to buy more stock, and that puts the price up. Then he unloads stock on them to the extent that they will buy it.

In a day or two, the stock may drop back to less than one half of what it was selling at. If this "one-man" manipulator wants to buy any stock, he will give out a little unfavorable news, and he can get stock at his own price.

After that the news is good or bad according to whether the manipulator wants to buy or sell, but as a rule he has an abundance of stock that he wants to sell, and is continually giving out good news.

A few years ago there was a man operating in New York who promoted several companies and manipulated them in a large way. He is out of business now, but the same thing is still done in a smaller way.

It is our opinion that more money is lost by the public in manipulated stocks than in promotion stocks, and we read a great deal about the enormous losses in them. Promotions that are failures may be perfectly legitimate and conducted in the utmost good faith, but manipulations are nearly always for the purpose of swindling the public. However, the lure of them is so great many people cannot withstand the temptations of them even after they have been "trimmed" several times.

PART FOUR
TOPICS OF INTEREST TO SPECULATORS

CHAPTER XVI.
MARGINAL TRADING

Most people who trade in stocks buy on margin. The ordinary minimum margin is about 20% of the purchase price, because banks usually lend about 80% of the market value of stocks.

If you put up 20% of the purchase price of your stocks with your broker, he has to pay the other 80%, but he can do that by borrowing that amount from his bank, and putting up the stock as security. In this way brokers are able to handle all the margin business that comes to them, as long as money can be borrowed. Of course, there are some stocks that are not accepted by banks as collateral for loans, and you should not expect your broker to sell such stocks on margin. In fact, if he offers to do so, it looks as though he were running a bucket shop. See Chapter XVIII.

Many people think that buying stocks on margin is gambling and that people should not do it for that reason, but buying on margin is done in all lines of business, although it may not be known under that name. If you bought stock outright, but borrowed 80% of the purchase price from your banker to complete your payment for it and put up the stock with him as security, you would be buying on margin just the same.

In like manner, if you bought a home and paid 20% with money you had and borrowed the other 80% of the purchase price, you would be buying a home on margin. The principal difference is that when you buy from a broker on margin, one of the conditions of his contract is that he has the right to sell your stock provided the market price drops down to the amount that you owe on the stock, whereas if you borrow money on a home, it is usually for a certain specified time and the lender cannot sell you out until that time expires. However, in principle, there is very little difference between the two transactions.

Most margin traders do not put up sufficient margin. If you put up only the minimum margin, your broker has the right to call on you for more margin if the price of the stock declines at all. Unless you are fully prepared at all times to put up an additional margin when called upon, you should make smaller purchases and put up a heavy margin when you buy. The amount of margin depends upon the transaction, but we advise from 30% to 50%, and at times we advise not less than 50% margin on any purchase. In fact there are times when we advise not to buy stocks on margin at all.

Those who wish to be entirely free from worry should buy stocks when the prices are very low, pay for them in full, get their certificates, and put them away in a safe deposit box. However, when stocks are low the risk in buying on a liberal margin is very small, and the possibilities of profit are so much greater, we do not see any objection to taking advantage of this method of trading.

CHAPTER XVII.
SHORT SELLING

By short selling, we mean selling a stock that you do not possess, with the intention of buying it later. Short selling in general business is very common, and we think nothing of it. Manufacturers frequently sell goods that are not yet made, to be delivered at some future time. Selling stocks short is a similar transaction, except that in a majority of cases delivery of the stock must be made immediately.

However, your broker can attend to that by borrowing the stock. As explained in the preceding chapter, when the market is active most of the trading is done on margin. Your broker buys a stock for you, but as he has to pay for it in full, it is customary for him to take it to his bank and borrow money on it. A bank usually lends about 80% of the market value, but if some other broker wants to borrow this stock, he will lend the full value of it. If that particular stock is very scarce and hard to get, the lender of the stock may get the use of the money without any interest.

Therefore, there is an advantage to the broker in lending stock, and for that reason it is nearly always possible for a broker to arrange delivery of stock for you if you wish to sell short. When you instruct him later on to buy the stock for you, he will do so and deliver it to the broker from whom he borrowed it, who will return the money he received for it.

When you sell stock short and the price goes up, you will have to pay a higher price for it. Therefore, to protect himself against the possibility of losing, your broker demands a payment from you just the same as you pay margin when you buy stock.

Short selling is something that we do not recommend very much to our clients. We think it is not advisable to do any short selling as long as there are good opportunities to make money by buying; but when all bargains disappear, as they do sometimes, you must either sell short or else keep out of the market entirely. At such times, there may be many opportunities to make money by short selling, and we do not consider that there is any reason why our clients should not take advantage of them.

Of course, great care must be exercised in selling stocks short. You might sell a stock short because you know the market price is 100% greater than its real value, but it is possible for manipulators to force it up a great deal higher; and if you are not able to put up sufficient money with your broker to protect him, he will buy at a high price and you will lose the money you have put up with him. In some instances, stocks are cornered and the short interests are forced to buy the stocks at prices that represent enormous losses.

It is a common thing to read about the short interests in certain stocks. All stocks that are sold short must be bought sooner or later, and when that buying takes place, it may affect the market very much. Therefore, if it is known that there is a big short interest in a certain stock, we should expect the stock to sell at a higher price; but sometimes the short interests break the market and force the price down, especially when general conditions are in their favor.

CHAPTER XVIII.
BUCKET SHOPS

There has been so much publicity given to bucket shops, nearly everybody is familiar with the term. A broker runs a bucket shop when he sells stock to his clients on margin and either never buys the stock for their accounts, or else sells it immediately after buying it. The bucket shop simply gets your money on the supposition that you are more likely to be wrong than to be right. Of course, if you take the bucket shop's advice you surely are likely to be wrong. Bucket shops get their clients into the very speculative stocks, where there is likely to be a great deal of fluctuation in the price of the stocks, which gives them frequent opportunities to sell out their clients.

When the market is going down or when there are many movements up and down in the price of stocks, the bucket shops make money rapidly, but occasionally there is a long period when the market is working against the bucket shops, and unless they have a great deal of money they must fail.

In August, 1921, Stock Exchange stocks started to go up. The upward movement was very slow but it was continual. Up to the time of this writing, there has not been a three-point reaction, except in a few stocks, in all of that time. Without a fluctuating market, the bucket shop has no chance to clean out its customers. As a consequence, the bucket shops began to fail in the early part of 1922, and up to the present writing (April, 1922) there have been more than fifty of these failures. However, it is not likely that all the bucket shops will be put out of business. The more successful ones are likely to "weather the storm."

Many laws have been enacted against bucket shops, and we believe some way will be found to get rid of them at some future time; but we do not expect that to happen soon, and we warn our readers not to get into their hands, because if they do not get your money away from you one way they are likely to get it some other way. The man who runs a bucket shop usually has no conscience, and it certainly is an unfortunate thing for anyone to get mixed up with such a man.

CHAPTER XIX.
CHOOSING A BROKER

It is very important that you choose a good broker. No matter how careful you are, it is possible to make a mistake. However, if you choose a broker who is a member of the New York Stock Exchange, you have eliminated a very large percentage of your chances of getting a wrong broker.

Occasionally a member of the Stock Exchange fails and once in a while one is suspended for running a bucket shop or being connected with one, but these instances are very rare compared with the number of brokers who get into trouble who are not members of the New York Stock Exchange. The rules and regulations of the Stock Exchange protect you to a great extent.

When you buy stock on margin, you leave your money in the hands of a broker, and you should know that he is responsible. No matter who your broker is, you should get a report on him. If you are a subscriber to Bradstreet's or Dun's Agencies, get a report from them. If you are not a subscriber to any mercantile agency, you perhaps have a friend who can get a report for you, or your bank may get one for you. Banks make a practice of getting reports of this kind for their clients. When asked to do so, we send our clients the names of brokers who are members of the New York Stock Exchange, but we prefer not to recommend any broker. Of course, we cannot guarantee that a broker is all right. We simply use our best judgment, but, as we said before, you eliminate a large percentage of your chances of going wrong when you trade with a broker who is a member of the New York Stock Exchange.

CHAPTER XX.
PUTS AND CALLS

A "put" is a negotiable contract giving the holder the privilege to sell a specified number of shares of a certain stock to the maker at a fixed price, within a specified time. A "call" is the exact reverse. It is a negotiable contract giving the holder the privilege to buy a specified number of shares of a certain stock from the maker at a fixed price, within a specified time. The price fixed in a put or call is set away from the market price a certain number of points, depending upon the stock and the condition of the market. When the market is steady and not fluctuating, the price fixed is frequently only two points away, but in a more active market it is considerably more.

For instance, at the present time, U. S. Steel is selling at about 95, and you can buy a call on it at 97 or a put at 93. That is by paying a certain amount, which at present is $137.50, you can have the privilege of buying 100 shares of U. S. Steel at 97, within thirty days of the date of the purchase of your call. If Steel should go up to 101 you could have your broker buy it at 97 and sell it at the market, and you would make a profit of four points, less the cost of your call and commissions.

As a method of operating in the stock market, we do not recommend the buying of puts and calls. Professional speculators may be able to use them to advantage sometimes, but for the outsider, who is not in close touch with the market, there is nothing about them to recommend.

Here is one point: the people who sell puts and calls fix the terms. If the market is irregular, they will set the point of buying or selling far away from the market price. These people are shrewd traders and they make the terms in their own favor. It is generally said that nearly all the buyers of puts and calls lose, and that is our opinion. Therefore, we advise you to leave them alone.

CHAPTER XXI.
STOP LOSS ORDERS

A "stop-loss" is an order to your broker to sell you out if the market sells down a certain number of points. Many speculators place stop loss orders only two points from the market price. The idea is that when the market starts to go down it is likely to continue going down, and by taking a two-point loss you may save a much greater loss. It also can be applied to a short sale, when you give your broker instructions to buy in the stock for you if it goes up a certain number of points.

We read so much in the financial news about stop-loss orders or merely stop orders, which is the same thing, the average reader is likely to get the idea that it is something he must use for his own protection, but it is our opinion that it is something that should be used very seldom by those who trade along the broad lines recommended by us. If your purchases were made in stocks that were very cheap, you should continue to hold them in case of a reaction. If you bought them outright or on a substantial margin, you are not in danger, and you should look upon your loss merely as a paper loss. In the great majority of cases, you will be a great deal better off to hold on to your stocks than you would be if you had a stop-loss order.

A large number of stop-loss orders is a good thing for the short interests. Let us take U. S. Steel again, as an example. Suppose it is selling at 94 and it is believed that there are a large number of stop-loss orders at 92. The short interests may sell the stock heavily and force it down to 92. Then the brokers with stop-loss orders would begin to sell; that would force the price down still lower, and the short interests could buy in to cover at this lower price.

Therefore, we believe that stop-loss orders are a bad thing and, as a rule, do not recommend them.

There is one instance where a stop-loss order can be used to advantage, and that is near the top of a bull market. It is impossible to tell when the market has reached the top. If you sell out too soon, you may lose a profit of several points. Of course, it is better to do that than to take a chance of a large loss. In that case, you might instruct your broker to place a stop-loss order at two or more points below the market, and keep moving it up as the market price moves up. Then when the reaction does come, he will sell you out and prevent you from losing a large part of your profit. That is about the only instance where we recommend a stop-loss order, but we do recommend it to our clients sometimes, although seldom.

If the stock you own is selling at more than 100 we would suggest that you make the stop loss order at least three points from the market, but for stocks selling below 100, a two-point stop-loss order might be used. However, the number of points should be decided upon in each particular case. In the special instructions to our clients, we tell them when we think they can use a stop-loss order to advantage.

PART FIVE
CONCLUDING CHAPTERS

CHAPTER XXII.
THE DESIRE TO SPECULATE

It is said that the desire to speculate is very strong in the American people. That is why our country has made greater progress than any other country in the world, because progress is the result of speculation. We are not referring merely to stock speculations, but to the word in its broadest sense. Every new undertaking is a speculation.

An inventor speculates on what he is going to invent. Often such speculations result in losses, because many inventors, or would-be-inventors, never accomplish very much. They spend their money, time, and efforts, and probably live years in poverty, and then if the invention is not profitable, they are heavy losers. Many inventors spend the best years of their lives in poverty and never succeed. We hear a great deal about some of those who do succeed, but very little about those who fail—those whose speculations were unsuccessful—except when somebody accuses them of being crooks because they solicited money for the promotion of their inventions and did not succeed.

It is the same thing with every new business. It is purely a speculation. It is a common saying that 95% of commercial undertakings fail. We do not know that that statement is correct, but there is no question but that the number of failures is very great, which shows the great risk in going into a new undertaking. It is far greater than the risk involved in stock speculating when it is done in accordance with the advice given in this book.

Yet, there would be no progress without speculating of this kind. If those entering a new business would make a careful study of the venture before entering it, and would exercise greater care and judgment in conducting it, the number of failures would be very much less. The same thing is true of stock speculating. The failures in stock speculating are caused mainly by ignorance and greediness. Many people who would be satisfied with a fair return on their money in a business enterprise, think they ought to make a 100% profit in a few weeks in stock speculation.

There is something about stock speculation that appeals to the greediness and pure gambling instincts of people. In the chapter on Manipulation, we have told you how stock prices are put up and down. Some outsider accidentally buys one of these stocks just before the price starts up. In thirty days he has made several hundred per cent profit. He does not realize that it was purely accidental as far as he was concerned, and he tries to do the same thing again, and loses all of his profits and probably all of his capital as well.

A stock gambler (we use the word "gambler" to refer to a man who operates ignorantly) is watching a large number of extremely speculative stocks and suddenly notices one that takes a big jump in price. Then he says to himself, "If I only had bought that stock on a ten-point margin, I would have made several hundred per cent profit." He picks out another stock that some one tells him is going to do equally as well. He buys as much of it as he can and puts up all the money he has as a margin, but the price doesn't go up. Perhaps the price goes down and he loses his margin; but, it may remain almost stationary for a long period, sometimes for a year or more, and during all of this time, this man is worrying for fear he will lose his money. If he does not lose his money, it is tied up for a long time where he cannot use it to take advantage of real opportunities that come his way.

It does not pay to take big risks. That is true in stock speculating the same as in any other undertaking. Most speculators are keeping their minds all the time on the possibilities of profit and not thinking about the possibilities of losing.

If you want to be successful in stock speculating, there is one thing you must learn to do, and that is never to think about the big profits you might have made if you had bought such and such a stock, because the probabilities are you could not have afforded to take the necessary risk in buying that stock.

Of course, after it is all over, it may look to you as though the buying of that stock was a sure thing, but the buying of such stocks is never a sure thing. The risk always exists. There is an old saying, and we believe a very true one, that a man who speculates with the idea of getting rich quickly loses all his money quickly, but that the man who speculates with the idea of making a fair return on his money usually gets rich.

In our advice to our clients, we seldom recommend highly speculative stocks, because we consider the avoidance of loss more important than the making of profits. You may object to that statement, because you speculate to make profits, and not for the purpose of avoiding losses. Nevertheless, if you are careful in keeping your losses down to a minimum, your profits are likely to be very liberal. Any trader who trades for any great length of time is likely to make large profits sometimes, and yet the majority of them have greater losses than profits. It is said that more than 80% of all margin traders lose; but we do not consider that an argument against trading on margin, because these losses are mostly due to ignorance, greediness, and the taking of too great chances.

Do not suppress your desire to speculate. All progress would stop if people did not speculate. But do not speculate in stocks nor in anything else without any knowledge of what you are doing, and try to use as much good judgment and care as possible in all of your transactions. If you do not know what to do, get advice from someone who is supposed to know and who is not interested in having you buy or sell. Stock speculating with safety is possible for those who make the effort to be guided by correct principles.

CHAPTER XXIII.
TWO KINDS OF TRADERS

There are two kinds of stock traders. One kind nearly always makes a profit, and the other wins sometimes and loses other times, but eventually loses all if he does not change his methods. The first kind buys stocks on liberal margin or outright and is not worried when the market goes against him, because he has good reasons for believing that prices eventually will go up. If he does have to take a loss occasionally, it is likely to be small compared with his profits. The second kind wants to make a big profit quickly, and he buys stocks that he thinks are going to make big gains in the near future, but his selections are not based upon good judgment.

We might designate these two traders as the careful trader and the reckless trader.

The careful trader tries to get good advice on the markets and the values of stocks. If the advice appears to him to be conservative, he is guided by it; but if the reckless trader gets advice on stocks, he is not guided by it if it is of a conservative nature. If he does take advice, it is likely to be from one of those unreliable market tipsters who is very emphatic in his statements about what the market is going to do. The reckless trader lets his greed and desire for large and quick profits influence his judgment.

Once in a while one of these reckless traders realizes that he has made a great mistake, and he wants to change his attitude. Usually he is holding several stocks that show a big loss and he does not know what to do with them. He reasons that they are selling so low now they surely will sell higher some time. Perhaps his reasoning is good and perhaps it is not. The stocks may have no chance of going up for a very long time, if at all, but even though they have a good chance to go up later, it is better for him to sell them now if he can put the money derived from the sale into something else that has a better chance to make a profit.

Our advice is never to hesitate to sell and take a loss if you can put the proceeds from the sale into something better rather than leave it in the stock in which it is now. It is not so much a question whether or not the stock you are holding will go up, as it is whether or not you would buy that particular stock if you were just coming into the market to make a purchase.

Of course there is a loss of commissions when you sell a stock and buy something else, and for that reason we sometimes recommend holding a stock when we would not recommend buying it.

If you have been a reckless trader in the past, the only thing for you to do is to change your methods and try to become a careful trader. It is much better to go to the extreme in carefulness and be satisfied with very small profits than to take great risks.

CHAPTER XXIV.
POSSIBILITIES OF PROFIT

What are the possibilities of profit in stock speculation? That question is frequently asked but it is difficult to answer. James R. Keene is quoted as having said: "Many men come to Wall Street to get rich; they always go broke. Others come to Wall Street to operate intelligently for fair returns; they usually get rich."

While it is true that nearly all stock traders who try to make unusually large profits in a very short time in stock trading lose, yet unusual profits can be made if you exercise good judgment and have patience.

Roger W. Babson, in his book entitled, "Business Barometers," speaks of the possibilities of profit in language that would be considered greatly exaggerated if used by a promoter, and yet he is extremely conservative in his advice to traders. He advises never to buy on margin, never to sell short, and staying out of the market entirely, neither buying or selling, for a great part of the time. Here is a quotation from his book, which follows a detailed statement of an investment of $2,500 over a period of fifty years:

"The preceding example shows that $2,500 conservatively invested in a few standard stocks about fifty years ago would today amount to over $1,000,000. These are not only strictly investment stocks, but are also stocks which have fluctuated comparatively little in price. This, moreover was possible by giving orders to buy or sell only once in every three or four years.

"If other stocks which were not dividend payers and which have shown greater fluctuations were purchased, and advantage had been taken of the intermediate fluctuations, the $2,500 would have amounted to much larger figures. By intermediate movements is not meant the weekly movements which the ordinary professional operator notes, but the broader movements extending over many months and possibly a year or more. Nevertheless, these broader intermediate movements should not be noticed by a conservative investor, as it is possible to correctly diagnose only the movements extending over longer periods. Many brokers believe that it is possible to discern also these intermediate movements of six or eight months; and if so, the following results would have been possible.

"$5,000 invested in 'St. Paul' in 1870 would amount to over $10,000,000 today.

"$5,000 invested in 'Union Pacific' in 1870 would amount to over $15,000,000 today.

"$5,000 invested in 'Central of New Jersey' would amount to over $30,000,000 today.

"$5,000 invested in 'Northern Pacific' would amount to over $50,000,000 today.

"These figures are not based on the supposition that the investor was selling at the top of every rise or buying at the bottom of every decline, but that the transactions were made at average 'high' and average 'low' prices based upon the study of technical conditions."

If such large profits can be made by following Babson's advice, of course larger profits can be made by buying on conservative margin and by selling short when all the conditions are in favor of it.

While there are possibilities of making extremely large profits without taking great risks, by those who are patient and exercise good judgment, one should be satisfied with a small profit, if it is the result of great care, in an effort to eliminate risk. Of course, you can afford to take a much greater risk with a small part of your speculative fund than you can with all of it. The less money you have with which to speculate, the more careful you should be. Some people cannot afford to speculate at all. They should invest their funds in good, safe investments, but this book is written for speculators.

Careful stock speculation carried on regularly over a period of years, we believe brings larger returns than almost anything else, and in the next chapter we tell you something about where to get information to guide you.

CHAPTER XXV.
MARKET INFORMATION

Where do you get your market information? Perhaps most people get it from the daily papers. When you look over the financial news of one of the leading metropolitan papers and see how much there is of it, you can get some idea of the enormous volume of work necessary to get this matter ready for the press in a few hours. There is no time to confirm reports. It is necessary that many of the articles be written from pure imagination, based on rumors.

Weekly and monthly periodicals can be more accurate in their information, but even they are not always dependable. Much of the financial news published comes from agencies that are not reliable. Read what Henry Clews says about them:

"Principally among these caterers are the financial news agencies and the morning Wall Street news sheet, both specially devoted to the speculative interests that centre at the Stock Exchange. The object of these agencies is a useful one; but the public have a right to expect that when they subscribe for information upon which immense transactions may be undertaken, the utmost caution, scrutiny and fidelity should be exercised in the procurement and publication of the news. Anything that falls short of this is something worse than bad service and bad faith with subscribers; it is dishonest and mischievous. And yet it cannot be denied that much of the so-called news that reaches the public through these instrumentalities must come under this condemnation. The 'points,' the 'puffs,' the alarms and the canards, put out expressly to deceive and mislead, find a wide circulation through these mediums, with an ease which admits of no possible justification. How far these lapses are due to the haste inseparable from the compilation of news of such a character, how far to a lack of proper sifting and caution, how far to less culpable reasons I do not pretend to decide; but this will be admitted by every observer, that the circulation of pseudo news is the frequent cause of incalculable losses. Nor is it alone in the matter of circulating false information that these news venders are at fault. The habit of retailing 'points' in the interest of cliques, the volunteering of advice as to what people should buy and what they should sell, the strong speculative bias that runs through their editorial opinions, these things appear to most people a revolting abuse of the true functions of journalism."

Of course, every trader gets market letters from one or more brokers. These are many and varied in character. Some of them are prepared with great care and give reliable information, but you must remember that a broker's market letter is published for the purpose of getting business, and business is created only by the customers' trading. Therefore it is to the broker's interest to have his customers make many trades instead of a few trades. In his book "Business Barometers," Roger W. Babson reproduces a letter written to him by the Manager of the Customers' Room of a Stock Exchange House. We consider this letter so important to all traders, we are taking the liberty to reproduce it here:

"Hearing on every hand about the fortunes made in Wall Street, I decided, upon being graduated from college, to devote myself to finance. With this end in view, I secured a position with a first-class New York Stock Exchange House, finally becoming the 'handshaker' for the firm; that is, 'manager' of the customers' room. So I had an exceptional opportunity to size up the stock business. The chief duties of the manager are to meet customers when they visit the office, tell them how the market is acting, the latest news from the news-tickers and the gossip of the Street. But the real duties are to get business for the house. Once a most peculiar man came to the office. He was about forty-five years of age, dressed in a faded cutaway coat, high-water trousers, and an East Side low-crown derby hat. In a high squeaky voice he said that he knew our Milwaukee House and would like to open an account. Of course, we were all smiles, for here was a new 'customer.'

"One day while in Boston he called us up on the long-distance telephone to make an inquiry about the grain market. One of my assistants, desiring to get a commission out of him, said 'We hear that Southern Pacific is going up; you had better get aboard.' He said 'All right; buy me a hundred at the market.' The stock was bought, but he never saw daylight on his purchase, for the market declined steadily afterward and by the time he got back from Boston it showed a heavy loss. The man who advised its purchase had no special knowledge about the stock, but simply took a chance, knowing that the market had only two ways to go, and it might go up, in which case, besides making twenty-five dollars in commissions for the house, he would be patted on the back for his good judgment. If the market went down, as it did, he would still make twenty-five dollars.

"I venture to say that 99% of the speculations on the New York Stock Exchange are based on such so-called 'tips'. The manager has got to get the business to keep his position and salary, and this can only be done by 'touting' people into the market. So he draws on the 'dope' sheets of the professional tipsters and his own feelings, and gives positive information to the bleating lamb that the Standard Oil is putting up St. Paul, or that certain influential bankers are 'bulling' Union Pacific. The lamb buys the stock, the broker gets the commission, and then the lamb worries his heart out as he sees his one-thousand-dollar margin jumping around in value. Now it has increased to eleven hundred dollars, then declined to nine hundred and fifty dollars, then nine hundred dollars, eight hundred dollars, then back to eight hundred and fifty dollars and then it takes the 'toboggan' to three hundred dollars upon which the broker calls for margins, and sells the customer out if they are not forthcoming, the whole speculation being based on the manager's 'feeling' that stocks ought to go up.

"Men of affairs who will not play poker at home, and are shocked at the mention of faro and roulette, which any old-timer will tell you are easier to beat than the stock market, think they are using business judgment when they try to make money on stock market 'tips'. Anyone with common sense can see that a 10% margin has no more chance in an active market than a brush dam in a Johnstown flood. One of the causes for this kind of speculating on a margin is that a broker's commission is only 12 1/2 cents per share and it does not pay to do small-lot business. The one-thousand-dollar margin would only buy ten shares outright and net the broker but $1.25 for buying and $1.25 for selling, whereas that same amount as margin on one hundred shares yields the broker $12.50 each way besides interest on the balance, the net result being that for any given amount of money a speculator on 10% margin multiplies his profits by ten and his losses by ten over those that would occur were he to buy the stock outright and take it home. The broker on his side multiplies his commission by ten over what he would receive were he to do an investment business."

From the above letter you get an idea of the attitude of an employee of the average broker's office. He would not be considered loyal to his employer if he had a different attitude. When an attitude like this influences the broker's market letters, they are not reliable.

You may ask whether there is any reliable information about the market. Yes, there is. There are several large organizations that make a study of fundamental statistics and statistics of different companies and give information to their subscribers based upon this knowledge. We believe that is the only kind of information that is worth very much to a trader, except the statistical information—the number of shares sold and the prices at which they are sold—he gets from his daily or weekly papers. Some of the principal organizations of this kind are as follows:

Standard Statistics Company, Inc.
Babson's Statistical Organization.

The Brookmire Economic Service.
Harvard Economic Service.
Poor's Investment Service.
Moody's Investors Service.
Richard D. Wyckoff Analytical Staff.

The above are the principal organizations of this kind. Subscriptions to their service cost from $85 to $1000 a year. In addition to these there are a few other organizations besides our own and individuals giving a somewhat similar service, but we know of none that gives such a service at as low a price as ours.

You should not confuse the service given by the above organizations with that given by many organizations and individuals who attempt to tell you what the market is going to do from day to day. In other words, they give 'tips' on the market. There are a number who issue daily market letters of this kind and charge from $10 to $25 a month for their service, but it is a line of service that we do not recommend at all, because we consider that you would be taking a very great risk if you followed advice of that kind. You might make enormously large profits occasionally, but you would also have frequent losses, and when the losses did come they might be greater than all the previous profits. We want you to understand that that kind of advice is entirely different from what we are recommending.

CHAPTER XXVI.
SUCCESSFUL SPECULATION

Success in stock speculation depends upon a few things that are very simple.

If you know what to buy, when to buy, and when to sell, and will act in accordance with that knowledge, your success is assured. You may think it is impossible to know these things, but it is not so difficult as it is supposed to be.

Many people buy stocks at the wrong time, and most of those who do buy them at the right time, buy the wrong stocks. Right now (early in April, 1922) is buying time in the stock market, and it is possible that this buying time may continue—with some interruptions—for another year or two, or even longer.

It is more difficult, however, to tell you WHAT stocks to buy. First of all, we advise you against buying stocks that are put up to high prices by manipulation. Of course, if you get in one of those stocks right and get out right, your profits are very large, but you take a great risk, and those who win once or twice by this method are almost sure to lose everything sooner or later in an effort to do the same thing again. Your chances are not much better than if you gambled at Monte Carlo. The chances in buying manipulated stocks are invariably against the outsider.

There always is so much publicity about these very active speculative stocks that the public is attracted towards them. Newspapers and brokers' market letters give altogether too much space to them. Such stocks sell far too high, and when the break comes, it brings ruinous losses to many people.

On the other hand, by following a conservative course, you really have a chance to make large profits with a minimum risk. We are giving below sixteen stocks that we recommended in our Advisory Letter of February 14th, 1922, with the approximate prices of them then and the approximate prices on March 31st.[2] In arriving at these prices, we took the closing prices on February 13th and on March 31st, and omitted the fractions. We recommended only sixteen stocks on that date, and you will see that every one of them made substantial gains.

Stock	Approximate Price Feb. 14, 1922	Approximate Price Mar. 31, 1922	Profit

C. R. I. & P. pfd (6)	75	79	4
C. R. I. & P. pfd (7)	88	93	5
New York Central	76	88	12
Pacific Gas & Electric	64	68	4
Consolidated Gas	90	109	19
American Telephone & Telegraph	118	121	3
General Motors Deb. (6)	70	78	8
General Motors Deb. (7)	81	91	10
U. S. Steel	87	95	8
Dome Mines	23	26	3
Laclede Gas	50	63	13
Missouri Pacific Pfd	48	54	6
C. R. I. & P. Common	33	40	7
Am. Smel. & Refining	45	53	8
Anaconda	47	51	4
Erie Common	10	11	1
Total	1005	1120	115

Let us suppose you bought ten shares of each of these stocks on February 14th. They would have cost you $10,050. We recommended 30% margin on the first ten, all of which were dividend payers; and 50% margin on the last six, because they were more speculative and would have been more affected by a reaction in the market. To buy ten shares of each on that margin basis would have required a little less than $3,500, but let us suppose you put up $3,500. After allowing for buying and selling commissions and interest on the balance of $6,550, but crediting you with dividends paid, your profit would be about 32% or at the rate of about 250% per annum.

Of course, we do not claim that by following the conservative course we advise, you always will make such large profits, although you might do just as well as that if you took advantage of some of the opportunities so frequently to be found in the market; but keen discrimination in what you buy always is necessary. However, let us suppose you made annual profits of one-fifth the above amount, or 50%, which is easily possible without taking the risks that are usually taken in stock speculating. If you invested $1000 and made 50% profit per annum, reinvesting your profit at the same rate each year for twenty years, you would have more than THREE MILLION DOLLARS.

When there is a possibility of making such enormous profits as that by following careful methods, surely there is no argument in favor of taking the extreme risks that people do take in buying the highly speculative stocks, the prices of which are put up for the purpose of unloading them on the public. Ten of the stocks we selected in the above list were dividend payers, and while the other six were not, they were considered worth much more than their market prices, and the list as a whole was conceded by conservative people as a safe one to buy.

Very frequently we are able to recommend a list of stocks that we believe will yield equally large profits, but the stocks you should buy are not the ones that are the most active nor the ones that are mentioned most frequently in the financial news and brokers' market letters. The stocks that most people buy are usually the very stocks that should be left alone. The stocks you should buy are usually the ones you hear very little about.

There is only one SAFE way to speculate, and that is to be guided by a knowledge of the fundamental conditions of each stock and also of the industries they represent. There are several large organizations giving information of this kind, and those who have been guided by the fundamental statistics issued by them, almost invariably have made money in stock speculating. The value of that kind of service has been thoroughly demonstrated beyond any question. However, a subscription for the service of most of these organizations costs more than the average person can afford to pay. Usually it is anywhere from $100 to $1,000 a year.

We are giving a service for the purpose of guiding our clients to successful speculation for a fee of only $25 a year, $15 for six months, or $10 for three months. For this fee we tell you what stocks to buy, when to buy, and when to sell. We send you our recommendations at least twice a month, but send you additional Advisory Letters and lists oftener if conditions make it necessary. You also have the privilege of unlimited personal correspondence regarding your market problems. The cost of our Service is very small, compared with what other reliable organizations charge.

Our Service is based on the principles expounded in this book. We try to select stocks having the greatest possibilities of profit with minimum risk, and the sample of our Service given in this chapter is proof of our success.

FOOTNOTES:

[2] We did not advise the sale of these stocks on March 31st, but the author figured profits to that date because this book was written shortly after that. If these stocks had been bought on or about February 14th, on the margin basis suggested by us, and sold six months later, the profit would have been more than 60%, or 120% yearly.